What is...
?
Shiny

Heinemann

First published in Great Britain by Heinemann Library
an imprint of Heinemann Publishers (Oxford) Ltd
Halley Court, Jordan Hill, Oxford OX2 8EJ

MADRID ATHENS PARIS
FLORENCE PRAGUE WARSAW
PORTSMOUTH NH CHICAGO SAO PAULO
SINGAPORE TOKYO MELBOURNE AUCKLAND
IBADAN GABORONE JOHANNESBURG

© Heinemann Publishers (Oxford) Ltd

Designed by Heinemann Publishers (Oxford) Ltd
Printed in China

99 98 97 96 95
10 9 8 7 6 5 4 3 2 1

ISBN 0431 07977 3

British Library Cataloguing in Publication Data
Warbrick, Sarah
Shiny. - (What is...? Series)
I. Series
500

Acknowledgements
The Publishers would like to thank the following
for the kind loan of equipment and materials used in
this book: Comet, Harlow; Early Learning Centre, Bishop Stortford;
Malsens, Bishop Stortford; Salisbury's, Harlow.
Toys supplied by Toys Я Us Ltd,
the world's biggest toy megastore.

Special thanks to Katie, Nadia and Rose who appear in the photographs

Photographs: Bruce Coleman pp4, 6, 14-15, 16, 17; Stock File p10;
other photographs by Trevor Clifford
Commissioned photography arranged by Hilary Fletcher
Cover Photography: Trevor Clifford

There are shiny things all around us.
Shiny things can dazzle or glow.
Shiny things can help us see in the dark.

This book shows you what is shiny.

These things look different.
What differences can you see?

In one way they are all the same.
They are all shiny.

The sun shines because it
gives off light.

Why does the torch shine?

A glow worm also gives off its own light.

Why do the numbers on the
clock shine?

Some things shine because
light bounces off them.
We say that they reflect light.

The sea shines because it reflects light
from the sun or moon.

Cyclists wear clothes that shine
in the dark.

These firemen's clothes have
shiny strips.
Shiny clothes are safe at night.

Look at the boat.
The shiny lights help to
keep it safe at night.

Why do the lights on the
bridge shine at night?

The moon shines at night.

It reflects light from the sun.

This elephant isn't shiny when it's dry.

Why does it look shiny now?

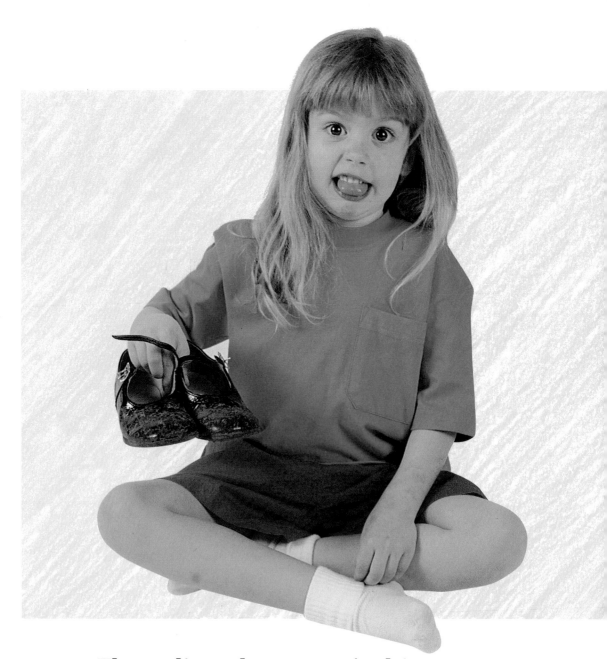

These dirty shoes aren't shiny.

But polish them and
you can see your face in them!

What is shiny here?

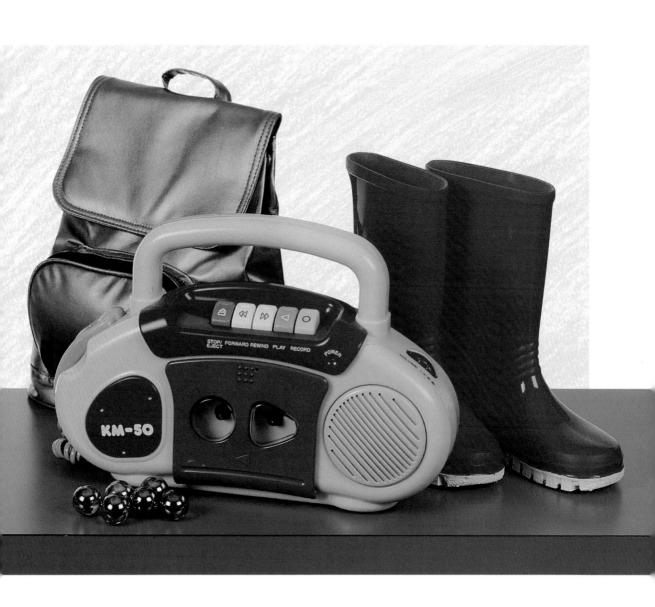

Index